The Union Steward's Field Book

A Pocket Guide to Dealing with Management

Randy A. Speeg

Eldurhara Books

The Union Steward's Field Book

Copyright © 2020 by Randy A. Speeg

Published by Eldurhara Books, an imprint of Sasgora Publishing.

EldurharaBooks.com

All rights reserved.

No part of this book may be reproduced in any form or by any electronic or mechanical means, including information storage and retrieval systems, without written permission from the author, except for the use of brief quotations in a book review.

Contents

Introduction	1
1. The Union Steward	2
2. Addressing Issues on the Job	4
3. Disciplinary Meeting Checklist	8
4. What Are Weingarten Rights?	11
5. Weingarten Rights: Questions & Answers	17
6. Just Cause for Discipline or Discharge	21
7. Be Aware of Management Ploys	23
8. What is a Grievance?	26
9. Writing a Grievance	28
10. To Be Made Whole	30
11. The Union Right to Information	32
12. Important Websites	36
13. Forms for Union Stewards	37

About the Author	39
Also by	40

Introduction

So you have decided to become a Union Steward. Congratulations on taking the initiative to lead and represent your fellow employees.

You will find that this job is both very rewarding, and can become very frustrating. Ensuring that your membership stays aware of their rights, and that Management adheres to the Collective Bargaining Agreement (the Contract) in all aspects of its day to day business, is a full time job. A job that in most cases you are choosing to do without additional compensation, all while also maintaining your regular job duties for the Company.

My goal in putting together this Field Book is to help provide you with the most important information you will need to fulfill your daily duties as a Union Steward, in a format that you can keep on hand and reference quickly.

1

The Union Steward

The union steward has the responsibility for protecting the rights of employees and for building a strong union workplace. In carrying out these responsibilities he/she has a number of duties.

1. Handle Grievances and administer the Contract.
2. Organize members and keep them informed.
3. Educate employees on their contractual rights.
4. Give leadership to the membership.
5. Assist employees with on-the-job problems.

In order to carry out these duties, he/she must know several things.

A. The Contract
B. The Union
C. The Company
D. The Department

E. The People

F. The Jobs

G. Labor Laws

H. Health and Safety Standards

I. Social Agencies

J. Legislative Issues

2

Addressing Issues on the Job

Stewards need to follow a specific procedure with respect to addressing issues on the job. The most important thing a steward can do is make himself/herself available to the members. Good listening skills save time and clarify the issues at hand. Here's a quick set of guidelines for stewards to follow as they listen to their members, investigate problems & concerns, and raise matters with company management. Work closely with your fellow stewards, officers, and employees on ways to be effective advocates for your union members and their families.

Investigation

1. Get the 5 W's: *Who, What, Where, When,* and *Why* of the problem. Be aware of contractual time limits.

2. Interview the grievant and determine what contract clauses may have been violated.

3. Interview the witnesses and get the relevant documents.

4. Re-evaluate the work problem after your investigation.

5. Discuss the strengths and weaknesses of the case with your Chief Steward or President.

6. Investigate every grievance as if it might go to arbitration.

Is It Grievable?

1. If the work problem is not grievable explain and discuss why with the grievant.

2. Discuss alternative ways to resolve the problem.

Put it in Writing

1. Write a simple, factual, brief description of the grounds for the grievance. It should answer clearly "What Happened?"

2. Cite the contract articles/sections violated and add "and all other relevant contract articles and rules."

3. Ask for a remedy and include, "and all other benefits to which the grievant is entitled."

4. Watch for opportunities to file group grievances, policy grievances, or union grievances.

Head Them off at the Pass

1. Cite every provision of the contract, which may have been violated.

2. The Employer must have "just cause" for disciplinary action.

3. Upon request, an employee is entitled to your presence at a management investigatory interview that could lead to discipline.

4. You have a Duty of Fair Representation.

Settlement

1. Find out the management's position.

2. Explore settlements (see Partnership).

3. Discuss the strength of the case and next steps with the grievant.

4. If an informal settlement is not reached, tell management a written grievance may be filed.

Partnership

1. Never settle a grievance without consulting the grievant.

2. Always get a grievance settlement in writing.

3. Don't miss a time limit while waiting for a settlement.

4. Be aware of any future precedents you may be setting.

Presenting

1. Follow the contractual time limits of your Contract at each step of the grievance process.

2. Never present the grievance without the grievant being there.

3. Keep copies of the grievance at each step and each written response. Keep notes of management's statements in grievance meetings.

4. You have a protected right to vigorously represent your members.

5. If employees want to handle their own grievances, the employer must notify you; you have a right to be present, and the adjustment must be consistent with the Contract.

3

Disciplinary Meeting Checklist

Be sure you remember all the things you're responsible for in a Disciplinary meeting (bring a copy of this checklist with you to the meeting to help you stay on track):

1. If you have advance notice, ask management what it's about. Then you can prepare yourself (and the employee) for the questions they'll ask.

2. What to tell the employee before the meeting:

- Be calm, cool, and collected.

- Be careful.

- Anything you say can be used against you.

- Keep answers short. Don't volunteer anything the Company doesn't already know. You can't refuse to answer, but you don't have to go out of your way to be helpful.

3. Your presence should inhibit management from browbeating the employee. If it doesn't, you can protest such behavior and include it in your notes.

4. You are taking careful notes on the whole meeting. (They'll be needed if the situation leads to further grievance steps.)

5. You can (during the meeting) give the employee advice on how to answer. You can also ask management to state the questions clearly, and request brief recesses to confer with the worker.

6. You're there to make sure the employee is treated fairly and to show that the Union stands behind them. Do that and you've done well.

Preventing problems before they start:

It's important to remind your members about their **Weingarten Rights**: Employees have the right to request a steward if a meeting could lead to discipline action or a potential Contract violation. Employees should always make this request for their own protection. Management is not required to notify employees of this right, but they can not deny this request once it has been made.

There may be times when management ignores an employee's Weingarten Rights request. Counsel your membership for these situations to do the following: stay in the room to hear the manager out; take detailed notes stating that he or she requested a steward and the request was denied; do not answer investigatory questions without a steward present; upon leaving the meeting contact a steward *immediately* to file a charge with the NLRB.

4

What Are Weingarten Rights?

The Employee's Rights During Investigatory Interviews with the Company

The National Labor Relations Act (NLRA) gives employees the right to assistance from union representation during investigatory interviews. Although not explicit in the Act, the right was declared by the US Supreme Court in 1975 in NLRB vs. J. Weingarten, Inc. The rules the court announced have since become known as the Weingarten Rights.

Employees sometime confuse the Weingarten Rights with the Miranda Rights. However there is a big difference between the two. Under Miranda Rights police who question criminal suspects MUST notify them of their right to remain silent and to have an attorney present during questioning. Under Weingarten Rights employers have NO OBLIGATION to inform the employees of their rights to union representation. The employee must ask for union representation in such meetings.

An investigatory interview occurs when:

1. Management questions an employee to obtain information, and

2. The employee has a reasonable belief that discipline and/or other adverse consequence may result from what he or she says.

Investigatory interviews relate to such subjects as:

- Absenteeism

- Accidents

- Compliance with work rules

- Damage to company property

- Drinking

- Drugs

- Falsification of records

- Lateness, poor attitude

- Poor work performance

- Sabotage

- Slowdowns

- Theft

- Violations of safety rules

Not every discussion with management is an investigatory interview. For example, a supervisor may speak to an employee about the proper way to do a job. Even if the supervisor asks the employee questions, this is not an investigatory interview as the use or possibility of discipline is remote.

However a routine conversation changes character if a supervisor becomes dissatisfied with an employee's answers and takes a hostile attitude. If this happens, the meeting becomes an investigatory interview and Weingarten Rights apply.

When a supervisor calls an employee to the office to announce a warning or other discipline that has already been decided it is not an investigatory meeting since the supervisor is just informing the employee of a previously arrived-at decision.

Such a meeting becomes an investigatory interview, however, if the supervisor asks questions that are related to the subject matter of the discipline.

Having a steward present can help in many ways. The steward can:

1. Serve as a witness to prevent supervisors from giving a false account of the conversation.

2. Object to intimidating tactics or confusing questions.

3. Advise (when appropriate) an employee against blindly denying everything. Thereby giving the appearance of dishonesty and guilt.

4. Help an employee to avoid making fatal admissions.

5. Warn an employee against losing his or her temper.

6. Raise extenuating factors.

The Employee's Rights under Weingarten are as follows:

1. The employee may request union representation before or during the interview. Remember, the company does not have to offer union representation, but they must provide it if you request it.

2. After the request, the employer must choose from among three options.

- Grant the request and delay questioning until the union representative arrives.

- Deny the request and end the interview immediately.

- Give the employee a choice of: (a.) Having the interview without representation (usually a mistake) or (b.) Ending the interview (best choice if no union steward is coming)

3. If the employer denies the request for union representation and questions the employee, it commits an unfair labor practice and THEN the employee may refuse to answer questions.

Although sometimes supervisors try to assert that the only function of a steward at an investigatory interview is to observe the discussion, in other words be a "silent witness," this is WRONG. The union steward has the right to counsel the employee during the interview and to assist the employee to present the facts.

Legal cases have established the following rights and obligations of the union steward:

1. When the steward arrives, the supervisor must inform the employee and the steward of the subject matter of the interview. For example: the type of misconduct which is being investigated. (The supervisor does not, however, have to reveal management's entire case.)

2. The steward can take the employee aside for a private pre-interview conference before the questioning begins.

3. The steward can speak during the interview. (But, the steward has no right to bargain over the purpose of the interview or to obstruct the interview.)

4. The steward can advise the employee not to answer questions that are abusive, misleading, badgering, confusing or harassing.

5. When the questioning ends, the steward can provide information to justify the employee's conduct.

You should advise all the workers that you represent of their Weingarten Rights, and give them the following statement to read to management BEFORE a discipline meeting starts:

"If this discussion could in any way lead to my being disciplined or terminated, or affect my personal working conditions, I respectfully request that my union steward be present at this meeting. Without representation, I choose not to participate in this discussion."

5

Weingarten Rights: Questions & Answers

Commonly asked questions about Weingarten Rights:

1. A steward sees a member being interviewed in the supervisor's office. Should he demand to attend?

Yes. Stewards have the protected right to be included in any interview that may result in an employee's discipline. However, if the employee refuses representation, the steward cannot attend.

2. Larry is being questioned about a workplace theft and is asked to provide information about his co-worker Roger, who is suspected. Should Larry have union representation?

Yes. Although Larry may not be guilty of the theft, his refusal to answer questions about it could result in discipline. Also, he may be disciplined should he have any knowledge about the theft. He has a right to have union representation.

3. Management asks an employee to submit to a urine test. Does Weingarten apply?

Yes and No. Since a urine test is not an investigatory interview, the employee does not have a right to union representation. However, management must allow the employee to consult with the union to decide whether or not to take the test.

4. Can management pressure an employee to drop a Weingarten request?

No. Management commits an Unfair Labor Practice when coercing employees to give up their right to representation.

5. An employee is called to his supervisor's office, but the steward is on vacation. Can that employee insist that an interview be delayed until the steward's return?

No. If a union representative is not available, another representative or employee can be substituted. However, if the employer is responsible for that representative not being available, then the supervisor must end the meeting until the representative is available.

6. I am a steward. If called in by my supervisor to discuss a problem with my work, can I bring in my chief steward?

Yes. Stewards are covered under Weingarten just like any other employee. If you have a reasonable fear of discipline or other adverse consequences, you too are entitled to representation.

7. Can an employee ask for a lawyer during an investigatory interview?

No. Weingarten Rights only apply to union representation.

8. The plant manager telephones a member at home to ask about missing tools. Does the member have to answer?

No. Weingarten Rights also apply to telephone interviews. An employee fearing discipline can refuse to answer without union consultation.

9. A manager denies an employee his/her Weingarten Right, yet continues to ask questions. Can the employee just walk out?

In Some Cases. If the manager consistently denies the request, the employee may leave to get a steward, but not if the manager asks the employee to wait until a steward arrives.

10. Can Weingarten be invoked during a polygraph examination?

Yes. An employee may be represented during the pre-examination as well as the test itself.

11. Can management order an employee to open their locker without a steward present?

Yes. Locker (as well as car and handbag) searches are not interviews, so Weingarten does not apply.

12. If an employee is asked to sign an acknowledgment upon receiving a warning slip, must management allow union representation?

No. The employee is not being interviewed; in fact, the employee has already received discipline.

6

Just Cause for Discipline or Discharge

The following 7 questions are used to determine Just Cause.

A NO answer to any ONE or more of the following questions normally signifies that Just Cause and/or Proper Cause did NOT exist.

Question 1. Did the Company give to the employee forewarning or foreknowledge of the possible or probable disciplinary consequences of the employee's conduct?

Question 2. Was the Company's rule or managerial order reasonably related to (a) the orderly, efficient and safe operation of the Company's business and (b) the performance that the Company might properly expect of the employee?

Question 3. Did the Company, before administering discipline to an employee, make an effort to discover whether the employee did in fact violate or disobey a rule or order of management?

Question 4. Was the Company's investigation conducted fairly and objectively?

Question 5. At the investigation did the Company obtain substantial evidence or proof that the employee was guilty as charged?

Question 6. Has the Company applied its rules, orders, and penalties evenhandedly and without discrimination to all employees?

Question 7. Was the degree of discipline administered by the Company in a particular case reasonably related to (a) the seriousness for the employee's proven offense and (b) the record of the employee in his/her service with the Company?

7

Be Aware of Management Ploys

These are some popular management tactics designed to frustrate you and your union. Managers might use them "tactically" during your Step 1 meeting, or "strategically" over the weeks and months of a grievance process. But they will use them. They always have.

STALLING

Probably the all-time favorite. By foot-dragging, management hopes you'll lose interest and go away. This is why the grievance steps have time limits, and why you need to write them down. (You did write them down didn't you?)

SIDETRACKING, WATER-MUDDYING

Like a magician who misdirects your attention, bosses love to bring up issues that are not related to the grievance you're dealing with. Don't let them sidetrack the issue at hand.

THREATS AND INSULTS

Crude, but often effective. Don't let management provoke you into losing your temper. If you have a grievant with you at a meeting, be sure they're prepared for this one. Call a caucus (outside of the room) if you think somebody's about to lose their cool (including you).

HORSETRADING

When several issues are on the table, management may offer you a "trade": win one, lose one. Don't fall for it. It's a sure way to lose the trust of your members, and it may expose you to fair representation claims down the road. Never risk your integrity to buy a "win." If you lose both grievances, so be it. If you should ever fall for a horse-trade, the management will demand a concession from the union for every agreement there after.

STONEWALLING

Like stalling, only worse. Sometimes they're bluffing, sometimes not. This is the tactic arbitrations are made from. The only way to find out is to invoke the time limits in your contract. That's why they're there. It's the union's job to move the grievance along.

8

What is a Grievance?

What is a Grievance?
A complaint about wages, hours, or working conditions.

What are the Sources of Grievances?

A. Violation of the Contract.

B. Unfair or discriminatory treatment for one individual or a group.

C. Violation of Labor Law.

D. Violation of clearly established past practice.

Other Types of Complaints (Non-Grievable)

A. "Bad" Grievance (unlikely to win)

1) Personal difficulty between employees

2) Difficulty related to wages, hours, and conditions that the Company cannot control and do not violate the Contract.

B. No Grievance – No violation of the Contract or any past practice, and no discrimination or law violation that the Company can control.

9

Writing a Grievance

Numbering the Grievance:

Number the Grievance with your initials and the ordered number (or date) of your Grievance. This helps to track grievances over time and makes it easier to reference specific grievances in correspondence.

Example: **RS-001** or **RS-10-31-20**

Nature of Grievance:

1. List the Articles and Sections of the Contract that are involved, and always add the following text afterward: **"Any and all related Articles or Sections that may apply."** This will protect you should another part of the Contract be discovered to apply at a later time.

2. List the issue or issues involved (dates, times, people involved, remember the five "Ws"). If your union uses pre-printed

forms and you need additional room to explain the issue or issues involved simply attach another page.

Relief Sought:

List the Adjustment the Union is seeking.

Examples:

A. If the Employee has suffered a loss in benefits or wages. Use the following language:

"Reimburse the employee for (Wages lost, Insurance Benefits lost, Attendance Bonus lost, etc., etc.)"

But always add the following:

"Make the Employee Whole." or **"Make the Bargaining Unit Whole."** if the grievance affects the entire workforce.

B. If the Company has denied an employee or group of employees any other contractual benefit, be specific as to the benefits lost (Seniority, job biding, FMLA Leave, etc.), and always add the following language.

"Stop This Practice Forthwith."

Or

"Cease and Desist Immediately."

10

To Be Made Whole

The following is only a list of examples that can be included in the term "To Be Made Whole," and is not intended to be all-inclusive and/or restrictive as it pertains to any/and all wages, and benefits the Grievant or Grievants may be eligible for:

- **All Lost Wages**

- **Incentive Payments**

- **Holiday Pay**

- **Shift Differential**

- **Missed Overtime**

- **Insurance Premiums**

- **Vacation**

- **Seniority Privileges Restored**

When processing a Grievance related to the discharge, discipline or loss of any monetary Benefit of any employee, the Union Representative should always add the following when determining what adjustment or resolution the Union is asking for pertaining to a Grievance:

"Make the Grievant(s) Whole."

Or

"Make the Local Union Whole."

Or

"Make the Bargaining Unit Whole."

11

The Union Right to Information

There may be times where you will need to acquire information from the Company to aid you in the investigation or processing of a grievance. The NLRA allows the Union the right to obtain information from employers. This right is not explicit in the NLRA, however the Supreme Court has construed it from the requirement in Section 8(d) that employers and unions bargain collectively. Without access to information, the Union cannot fulfill its responsibility to negotiate, monitor, and enforce labor contracts. The Company's refusal to provide information, or cause unreasonable delays in doing so, will violate Section 8(a)(5) of the NLRA.

As a union steward, you may request information to:
- ensure compliance with the labor contract

- investigate whether or not a grievance exists

- prepare for a grievance meeting

- decide if a grievance should move forward

- prepare for an arbitration hearing

- prepare for contract negotiations

The Union is entitled to examine a wide variety of records to investigate a grievance or prepare for collective bargaining negotiations. You may request relevant documents, data, and facts. Information is considered relevant if it might be useful to the Union or could lead to the identification of useful information.

Information requests should always be made in good faith. Your request must relate to contract administration or bargaining, and you must explain your reasons if asked. The Union can't use an information request for harassment or to conduct a random fishing expedition unrelated to administering contractual issues.

If the Company does not have the requested information, it must make a reasonable effort to obtain the information, including requests to third parties with whom it has a relationship.

The Company may not demand preconditions, such as an insistence that the Union not disclose the information to outside parties, unless the information meets a strict test of confidentiality.

Employers can not refuse an information request based upon the size of the required data, however they may bargain for reimbursement of any cost incurred.

Employers will often make many excuses to avoid supplying the Union with the information requested. Below are some examples of Company excuses that have been rejected by the NLRB:

- You can get the information from your members.

- The request is too large.

- The grievance has no merit.

- The information has been posted.

- The grievance is not arbitrable.

- You can subpoena the information to the arbitration.

- Past grievances were resolved without this information.

- The materials are privileged.

- We will only give the information if you agree to give us similar information from union records.

- No documents exist under that titleholder.

- We will provide the information to the union if the grievance goes to a higher step.

- The grievance is time-barred.

If the Company refuses an information request without acceptable reasoning (such as employee medical confidentiality, confidential company trade secrets, etc.) then the Union should file a ULP charge with the NLRB.

If you should ever be required to file a charge with the NLRB, <u>DO NOT</u> also file a grievance regarding the issue of the charge (i.e. refusal to provide information). Doing so will cause problems as the NLRB will defer your charge back to the grievance procedure of your contract rather than issue a direct order to the Company to comply.

12

Important Websites

The below listed Federal Agencies and Labor Organizations are here to protect your rights as a Union Worker. If you contact them you can request to remain anonymous regarding any action taken by them on your behalf.

National Labor Relations Board (NLRB): www.nlrb.gov

Department of Labor: www.dol.gov

Occupational Health & Safety Administration (OSHA): www.osha.gov

American Federation of Labor & Congress of Industrial Organization (AFL-CIO): www.aflcio.org

Your own union may or may not be a member of the AFL-CIO, even if it is not, their website is a good source of valuable information.

13

Forms for Union Stewards

The following are downloadable PDF forms that you will find useful in fulfilling your duties as a Union Steward. Feel free to save these forms and share them with your fellow stewards and officers.

Downloadable Forms:

Disciplinary Meeting Fact Sheet:
https://www.dropbox.com/s/1epkco7q3pmy06h/DisciplinaryMeetingFactSheet.pdf?dl=1

Steward Investigation Form:
https://www.dropbox.com/s/hfh22qankwwud85/StewardInvestigationForm.pdf?dl=1

Grievance Log Sheet:

https://www.dropbox.com/s/kuc4vvwld46wz3k/GrievanceLogSheet.pdf?dl=1

Information Request Form:

https://www.dropbox.com/s/oc1rrdduarekx4h/InformationRequestForm.pdf?dl=1

About the Author

Randy A. Speeg has been Unit Vice President of the International Chemical Workers Union Council of the United Food and Commercial Workers International Union (ICWUC/UFCW) Local 664C since 2006, serving the employees of the Totes Isotoner Corporation in Cincinnati, Ohio.

Also by
Randy A. Speeg

The Union Steward's Pocket Guide to Negotiating: Be Prepared at the Bargaining Table

www.ingramcontent.com/pod-product-compliance
Lightning Source LLC
Chambersburg PA
CBHW050317220526
45465CB00005B/2031